LAURINDA JORDAN

SOUL RETRIEVAL

**The Ultimate Guide to Spiritual Healing
For Your Soul, Discover How You Can Use
Spirituality to Heal Emotional Scars**

Descrierea CIP a Bibliotecii Naţionale a României
LAURINDA JORDAN
   SOUL RETRIEVAL. The Ultimate Guide to Spiritual Healing For Your Soul, Discover How You Can Use Spirituality to Heal Emotional Scars / Laurinda Jordan – Bucharest: Editura My Ebook, 2021
   ISBN

LAURINDA JORDAN

SOUL RETRIEVAL

The Ultimate Guide to Spiritual Healing For Your Soul, Discover How You Can Use Spirituality to Heal Emotional Scars

My Ebook Publishing House
Bucharest, 2021

TABLE OF CONTENTS

FOREWORD

Heartache and mourning are among the most thought-provoking experiences each of us has to face at one time or another in our life. If you come away from this book with only one thing, I hope you come to comprehend that you are able to be gentle with yourself as you move through the complex stages of emotional wounds.

With better understanding of the grief process, that is essential to heal emotional wounds, and learning the tools and skills you'll learn in this book, you'll discover you're able to markedly lessen your pain and suffering as you move through the process of healing emotional wounds.

The great news is that when faced with the inevitable, we might find ourselves undergoing intense emotions that we never imagined we would or may feel. And these emotions may be cleansing - providing dismissals from attachments and memories that are no longer possible to resolve with an individual.

The further great news is that we might experience enormous emotional and spiritual growth in our journeys through heartache and mourning. Learning to experience and separate our sadness, angers and guilts that are aspects of the normal grief experience may be enormously beneficial in the long haul.

The foul news is that these are frequently painful experiences, which we may rather choose to avoid - if we'd the choice. These inevitable and inescapable challenges along the road of life might, however, be so painful that we can't ignore them. When we do push them away or detour around them, we might find that we're emotionally and physically debilitated and that these burdens of heartache are increasingly hard to bear. It may be ever so tempting to bury and brush aside these troublesome notions. While this might be at occasionally in our lives a necessary reaction in order to conduct our duties and responsibilities, if not with a battle for survival, it's a reaction that's fraught with a lot of risks.

Heartaches that are buried often develop into emotional time bombs that may become progressively dangerous to our normal lives, on a lot of levels of our beingness. It calls for

8

considerable effort to keep the uninvited feelings and memories hidden outside our witting awareness. This is a drain on our energies. We likewise protect ourselves by heading off relationships and spots that resonate with the wounds, unsolved grief experiences - our unconscious always on the job lest issues and feelings in the current spot resonate with the swallowed materials and activate a bomb that it fears will be overpowering. Our lives might become constricted and narrowed as a result of these defensive maneuvers.

Other divisions of our unconscious comprehend that these buried bombs are an unhealthful burden to be carrying around with us. Signals are sent from healing regions of our unconscious to draw our attention to the immersed feelings and memories that need clarification. These signals might include disruptive dreams, physical symptoms, or strange, excessively strong responses to assorted triggers in our currentlives.

In this e-Book you are able to explore a lot of avenues for dealing with challenging psychological and physical trouble through holistic affirmations for self-healing. You might choose to live your life in fresh and exciting ways. Your symptoms and issues need not be curses to be eradicated. Utilizing medications to deal with symptoms of grief and bereavement might in effect be a way of shutting up the messenger who's bringing you uncomfortable news that something inside you is out of sync, or a process to deadenyour reactions to these messages.

This brings you is a remarkable fresh method for easing your way through the process. While it might seem to you that the lightening of your burden is a hard challenge, a lot of grateful users report it's completely metamorphosed their process andtheir lives.

Spiritual Healing For Your Soul

Heal your emotional wounds and take control of your life.

Chapter 1

An Opportunity For Growth

Synopsis

Past wounds and Grieving about them frequently stops us in our tracks. The acute hurt, depression, anger, shame and additional feelings force us into self-contemplations and introspections that we'd otherwise prevent. This in itself is mending us, forcing us out of our childhood patterns of warding off painful emotions and escaping from them.

Viewing It Differently

The skills we memorize and the resources we gain in dealing with these feelings will carry on standing us in good stead with later experiences of acute emotions of all types.

When going through our healing of wounds we likewise have an excellent chance to clear our inner 'file drawers' where aged, disregarded, buried matters are stored beside the fresh ones. These techniques are especially helpful in this respect, enabling us to decrease the strength of residual notions from old grief along with new, raw feelings from the fresh ones.

We likewise learn compassion by our own experiences of sufferings. This is generally acknowledged in the observance that many of the better caregivers for ill people are themselves injured healers. Closure isn't a time or date when you shut the door on your wounded feelings and feel it no longer. Closure begins the instant you soak up the fact that the situation happened. With each step along the path of healing wounds you take is a step toward further, deeper closure.

Several are led astray to feel they've reached an early end to their closure when they're in the grasp of waves of sorrow, anger and shame of the moment. Learning that healing has its own method, its own timing and its own meandering, hilly road toward ever better closure is a part of the process. It's an awareness regarding the procedure of grieving and healing; a growing intimacy with how your mind and feelings react and deal with emotional wounds.

Heartache over our losses and wounds stops us in our tracks. It assists us in realizing a lot of disregarded truths and to acquire manyhelpful and life-enhancing lessons.

If you trust in endurance of the spirit and that you are able to recover, you might have fewer anxieties and even reach a place of much richer and greater admiration for all of the chances, blessings and lessons you've had and will have in this life. You'll pull through the closure process with Appreciation for the great experiences you recall and the lessons acquired; with gratefulness for the enrichments accumulated in your life so far; and with acute anticipation for the graces yet to come.

In this life there is transience in all experiences. Recognizing an end will bear on every and each relationship we have, including the elemental end of our relationship with all we have lived in this life, helps us to treasure every experience a great deal more. This awareness might be one of the biggest benefits of transitioning through the healing process.

Once we come through such grave challenges, other issues in our life shrivel up in comparison. As we clean-cut issues and feelings in the present tense, we frequently discover like issues lurking in the same file drawers. These might have been stacked away many years before, at times when we didn't bear the resources to handle them.

At present, with the successes of managing problems of grief and healing, you can do an exhaustive clearing up of such unnecessary baggage that you carry with you in your unconscious. This is the acceptance of grief as a part of healing; as that which bestows deep meaning to life; as a chance for clarifications; and as the terrificteacher it may be.

This is a branching out of our positive cognizance. That is, when we understand we're safe and need not fear our past experiences - which is for a lot of people very difficult- then all additional stress and fears in our lives become nothing more than added lessons. We understand that everything in our lifetime is manageable; there's nothing we haveto worry about or fear.

We may than accept everything in our life as a lesson. Rather than saying, "Oh, my goodness! How will I handle this challenge?" we can state, "Hmmm! I"m curious what intriguing lessons I'll get from this invitation to look deeper inside myself?" or "I question what I'll discover to clear up next from the file drawer that this hurdle is directing me towards?"

Chapter 2

General Healing

Synopsis

We all allow a small child plan our lifetime processor. Having made this inevitable mistake, we wind up making the goofy error of running these programs for nearly all of our lives. As youngsters, we frequently can't comprehend the causes for awful or frightening states of affairs. Youngsters can't alter their objectionable circumstances, can't leave, can't fire or switch out their parents. We're stuck in sadness and from our kid views, see no means out. In such spots, it's really helpful for us to head for the hills to hide from the hurt or to blank it out – burying the feelings externally of conscious awareness.

As youngsters, this is a great choice for warding off pain and suffering, as we can't prevent it. Following, our unconscious rapidly gets used to protecting us from the hurt of these hidden distresses by keeping them securely locked up so that we can't feel them and don't suffer from them. Feeling memories are stacked away in unconscious parts of the right side of the brain. The right hemisphere places a sign on the inner file cabinet stating, "Stand back!!" It addresses the more consciously aware left hemisphere and states, "We don't wishto understand about this, do we?" And the left hemisphere states, "nope, let's stand back from those dreadful memories and feelings." So we make-believe to ourselves they aren't there.

Understanding Helps Heal

Although this scheme works well to protect us as youngsters from concerns and pains, it shortly becomes the default for our lifespan inner „steering' programs. The unconscious stays afraid of these hidden feelings shut away in its file cabinet drawers. It trusts that the original, hidden concerns and hurts may still overpower us with all the strength of our original responses from the time when we immersed them.

As we become aged, these programs get old-hat. The unconscious, all the same working according to the youngster programs, doesn't understand we may manage these feelings better as grownups. For instance: The right hemisphere might warn us in small print below the „stand back' sign of the cupboard where concerns from our parents' arguments, tongue-lashings or other injurious behaviors are shut away. Such a sign might state, "Stand back from anything like arguments and from furious individuals."

We might thus prevent feeling disturbing emotions in our current lives (that unconsciously vibrate with our earliest life fears), but we likewise wind up blocking ourselves off from experiences and relationships that may have been much better managed or stomached when we're grownups. For example, we might avoid individuals with big voices or individuals who resemble our parents in additional manners.

Once we come across something in our current life that wakes thesemonsters in our closets, it's conceivable that the door to fearful memories may pop open a bit, and we may feel a few of the original, hidden feelings. This is why occasionally we over-react when an individual in our present life reminds us of somebody who scared orhurt us in the past.

I know someone who had a lot of anger toward his mother as a youngster, but swallowed it as she was a single parent and he didn'tfeel safe conveying it, and detected no other vents for it. For a long time, he was easily infuriated by authority figures, especially pushywomen.

As grownups, we go on to stuff uncomfortable feelings within ourselves, closing a mental door to keep them safely away from our awareness. Our unconscious mind watchfully stands guard over these emotions shoved away in files in the caverns of our being, stands firm against releasing them – still when we're no longer in the dreadful situations that caused them; still when we're clearly in a more beneficial position to cope with them.

For example, we may have hidden heartache, anxieties, fears and angriness when we were younger. It may begin with being distressed because our loved ones had to move; with one parent being forced to be away from home for an long period (for work or to look after issues of extended family); with heartache over our parents' splitting up; or with the demise of a loved one. If this sort of grief response were hidden instead of being conveyed, then we may wind up with an internal program that leads us to immerse all future grief responses.

As grownups, if we're once again grieving, we might feel very uncomfortable – totally out of proportion to what we're experiencing in the here and now. We might react with remarkably deep sadness or anger as the memories and notions are stirred in the cupboards holding our feelings from our earliest life. And so, what do we do?

18

Our chronic reaction is to stuff the fresh objectionable feelings into our inner cupboards, just like we did when we were too little to knowbetter.

With graver wounding experiences, like those of soldiers in wartime, the turning away might be more serious, followed by symptoms of post traumatic stress disorder. In addition to anxieties and sorrow, there might be flashbacks to the hurts; activating of acute fears or angers; irrepressible crying; grievous depression; trouble sleeping; intolerance for loud disturbances, closeness with others, and anythingelse that remotely resembles the traumatizing spot; and even self- destructive thoughts and demeanors. (It's usual for individuals with wartime PTSD to have had grave stresses and losses in earliest life.)

There might likewise be acute anxieties, due to the signs that discourage letting loose the hidden feelings and memories. It's reallyusual to feel that the acute, long-buried emotions may be overpowering – even as they felt during the original, wounding experiences.

The graver the abuse or harm has been, the more intense our responses might be to anything that trips the warnings on our file cabinet drawers and that conjures up the memories and feelings within them. Usual reports of such terrible traumas are connected to soldiers in combat zones, firefighters, policemen, emergency medical teams, victims of vehement crimes and assaults, survivors of child vilification, and others who were likewise abused or who saw such dreadful events.

Self-healing strategies and assorted therapies are available to free many of these well-buried and secret traumas, our internal programs commonly defy such efforts. Frequently, it's only if the emotional pus from past harms festers to the point of severe physical and emotional hurt that we even start to become aware that something disturbing is within us and come to recognize that it's begging us to free and deal with it.

When traumas have been grievous, it's often advisable and helpful to have the guidance and backing of a counselor or therapist who's trained in grief therapy – until individuals learn how to utilize these methods and till they acquire the confidence that the freed feelings and memories won't be overpowering.

Your negative, wounding memories can be transformed into profoundly healing and growth-enhancing experiences.

Chapter 3

Get Rid Of The Negative

Synopsis

Our childhood experiences frequently shape the balance of our lives. When we have endured neglect, physical or emotional harms, or ill-treatment, we frequently carry the burdens of hidden childhood emotions for decades after the issues. This is because we immerse the feelings deep below our witting awareness, frequently along with the memories, so that we don't go on as youngsters to suffer from them.

Stop Stuffing

While immersing these memories protects us as youngsters, this leaves us bearing a lot of buried 'material' that's stacked away in our unconscious and in our heart. Our unconscious youngster mind sets up platforms to prevent our being harmed by these hidden burdens: it leads us to stand back from anything similar to what we experienced - lest we hurt again as we had hurt before.

Our grownup experiences might leave us with damaging feelings likewise. We have all experienced things that we wish had never occurred. Who has not wanted to fix?

➤ Saying something in anger to loved ones, causing long-lived pain, disappointment or bitterness?

➤ Turning down a specific road, where an accident happened?

➤ Not saying something before a loved one or friend passed, when we hadn't said to them we love them, or shared something else of earnest importance?

There are assorted ways that we might become aware of our residual damaging beliefs and damaging habits. Occasionally, we simply get fed up with behaving in ways that are counter-productive to our current state of affairs and to our current wants. We awaken one day and recognize that 'it' is not just 'occurring' to us. We have to be acting in ways that ask for 'it' to happen.

Frequently it's our family and acquaintances who make show-stopping remarks or ask incisive questions, like: "How did you finaglefinding not just one or 2, but a series of 4 damaging individuals in a row – who all began appearing like such promising partnering material then turned on you and got abusive?" or "may there be anything in your presentations at work that's inviting all the critiques you've had? This is the 3rd position you've held where this has gotten to be an issue. May there be something in the way that you respond to individuals that rubs them the wrong way?" These might initially appear to us to be critiques, but when they're provided with love and care, and when we may see that our chronic behaviors wind up getting us counter-productive, uninvited reactions, we might pause long enough to review our habits that are precluding us from savoringand maximizing our potential in life.

When we start to have a look at our beliefs and conducts in such spots, we frequently discover that we have internal life-scripts that tell us such things as, "I don't merit love." We might have expectations like, "I'm certain they'll discover something incorrect with my presentation." or "The way to prevent being rejected for not being what individuals want me to be is to perform something that will get them to scorn me for what I don't do correctly."

When we grasp that things that we're feeling, trusting and behaving, it's really not that hard to make substantial shifts into better personal places. When we no longer anticipate rejection and failure, we're much less likely to act in ways that will bring us to that place which we fear.

If we discover ourselves blocked in our advancement in life or in our enjoyment of life, be it in our personal, relational, professional or spiritual lives, taking a close look may help us to change our negative notions and expectations. This then lets us alter our associated feelings and behaviors and to remold our ways of relating to ourselvesand other people.

Chapter 4

Using Spirituality

Synopsis

There are a number of Advantages to spirituality as it applies to healing emotional problems. These are found in this chapter.

Advantages And What To Use

By developing a spiritual connection, you gain security through the strong belief that you're not all alone in the universe, even at those times when you feel temporarily disjointed from others. You feel more and more safe as you come to trust that there's a source you areable to always turn to in times of trouble.

Serenity is the result of sensing a deep, enduring sense of security and safety. The more trust and reliance you develop in spirituality, the simpler it becomes to cope without fear or concern with the inevitable challenges life bestows. It isn't that you abandon your self or your will to such a power; instead you merely learn that you are able to "let go" and trust when you feel stuck with an issue and don't understand how to go forward. Learning how to relinquish when answers to issues aren't directly apparent may go a long way towards reducing worry and anxiety in your life. Serenity is what arises in the absence of such anxiety.

As you develop a spiritual relationship, you come to recognize that there's something great in you. You're part of the universe. You're great, lovable, and worthy of regard just by virtue of the fact that you're here. This fruition may improve the way you view yourself and will help you to better your ego and what you believe of yourself.

You're still inherently good and worthwhile. Your own judgings of yourself, however damaging, don't ultimately count if you're a creation of the universe as much as everything else.

The most cardinal characteristic of spirituality is that it provides you an experience of unconditional love. This is a sort of love which differs from romantic love or even average friendship. It means an absolute caring for the well-being of another with no conditions. That's, regardless how another individual seems or acts, you've compassion and treasure them without judging. As you acquire a deeper connection, you come to feel higher degrees of unconditional love in your life. You sense your heart opening more easily to individuals and their interests. You feel freer of judging them or of making comparisons amidst them. Unconditional love comes out both in your expanded capacity to give love to other people and to have more of it coming into your life. You start to experience less dread and more joy in your life and help to inspire other people to experience their own capacity for unconditional love. This sort of love in addition to manifests itself through the experience of having everything you require in your life to get on with what you wish to do.

Acquiring a relationship with spirituality will supply you with guidance for arriving at decisions and figuring out issues. Spirituality has a universal wisdom that goes beyond what you are able to accomplish through your own reason. In traditional faiths this has been referred to as the "divine intelligence." Through connecting, you are able to draw upon this higher wisdom to help you settle all kinds of troubles. By learning to invite guidance, you'll be surprised to discover that every sincere request eventually is answered. And the caliber of that answer commonly exceeds what you may have worked out through your own conscious intellect or will.

Abide by these guidelines for an effective relationship with spirituality:

1. Be calm, patient, and open.
2. Be positive that communication will happen.
3. Don't tempt or make terms. You must have uttered self-surrender as the price for the only true freedom that's worth having.
4. Be amenable to accept what is provided.
5. Invite help. Don't instruct on what to do.

These are a few of the characteristics that delineate a close relationship with spirituality. All of them may significantly add to your personal healing process. The extent and earnestness of your commitment will mold the degree of personal healing you experience. You are able to heighten your commitment to spirituality through anyof the following means:

1. Steady participation in church or your favorite spiritually basedorganization.
2. Steady reading of inspirational literature of your taste. It's goodto do this at any rate once per day, either upon waking up, during your lunch break, or before going to sleep.

28

3. Regular practice of meditation.

4. Steady practice of prayer or spiritual affirmations.

5. Acquire help from other people (Healing practicians, intercessoryprayer, etc.)

Wrapping Up

Spirituality may be viewed as being distinct from religious belief. Dissimilar world religions have proposed assorted doctrines and belief systems about the nature of a God and human beings relationship with it. Spirituality, on the other hand, bears on to the common experience behind these assorted viewpoints. It's an experience calling for an awareness of and relationship with something that exceeds your personal self as well as the mortal order of things. This "something" has been given assorted names ("God" being the plainest in Western Society) and delineated in ways that aretoo many to count. You are able to pick to define what that means foryourself in whatever way feels most advantageous. Your own sense of a God may be as abstract as "cosmic consciousness" or as earthy as the wonderful thing about the ocean or mountains. Even if you view yourself an agnostic or atheist, you might get a sense of aspiration from taking a walk in the forest or mulling over a beautiful sunset. Ora small youngster"s smile might give you a particular sense of joy and help with healing.

Printed by Libri Plureos GmbH in Hamburg, Germany